"THIS BOOK W ... SPIRITS OF MANY."
From the Foreword by Alan Clayton, Senior Pastor
The Ark Church, Conroe, Texas

FINISHING

WITH WHAT YOU HAVE LEFT

STRONG

Inspiring stories of people doing great things for God despite personal or physical challenges

RICHARD CLAYTON

Xulon PRESS

Editing: **Shelba Forrest**

Photography: **Aesthetic Images Photography**
            Greensboro, North Carolina

Additional Resources:

Howard E. Covington, Jr., *Making Disciples for Christ, A Businessman's Passion for His Church.* Copyright 2006, Royce Reynolds, Greensboro, N. C.

Ned Cline, *Building a Solid Foundation: The Al Lineberry, Sr. Story of Faith, Family, Educational Enhancements and Economic Development.* Copyright 2007, Gaines Corporation, Greensboro, N.C.

Bob Buford, *Finishing Well: What People Who Really Live Do Differently.* Copyright 2004, Integrity Publishers, a Division of Integrity Media, Inc., 5250 Virginia Way, Suite 110, Brentwood, Tennessee, 37027.

www.xulonpress.com

CONTENTS

FOREWORD

My father has always cast a large shadow. He's a big man, six feet four, broad shoulders, athletic, big smile. The quintessential all-American kind of guy. He's been successful as a husband, a father and a businessman. His focus, discipline, and drive have caused him to excel.

So I wondered how he would respond to the one thing he could not beat—tumors that appeared inside his spinal column and took away his ability to walk. I watched from a distance as he went from not being able to run, to slow unsteady walking, and then a cane, a walker, and finally, a wheelchair. However, in this time when his body forced him to sit, to me, he has stood the tallest.

My father's refusal to allow a disability to affect his spirit, his leadership, and his willingness to engage in life has been inspiring. I am sure he has had his moments, but he has shown a perseverance to push through the disappointment and reach out to touch and encourage others.

I believe this book will refresh and uplift the spirits of many. It was written from the perspective of a man who is determined to finish strong despite his physical setbacks. I am honored to write this foreword. I am more honored to be his son.

Alan Clayton
Senior Pastor
The Ark Church
Conroe, Texas

Introduction

This book is an outstanding collection of inspiring stories about real life people who have been dealt difficult blows in life. In one instance, you'll read about a man who lost his eyesight, yet continues to do remarkable things. Another story will tell about someone who lost his ability to walk, but continues to engage in life. Then there is the encouraging account of a federal judge who battled a deadly cancer for over five years. He made sure that those five years were a time of significance and a quality of living that were an amazing display of finishing strong. Read further and you'll be impressed by a grandmother's victory over Parkinson's Disease and a successful businessman saying no to two heart attacks and cancer.

Page after page, you'll be amazed at the indomitable spirit and the strong faith in God shown in these lives.

Whether you have been afflicted by a physical or mental problem, or whether you are young or older, this book should be a source of inspiration and courage and a mandate to finish strong with what you have left.

This book is dedicated to my beloved wife, Raydean

Thank you for being a wife after God's own heart so that I could grow into a husband after God's own heart.

Thank you for how you poured the Word of God into our children, Alan and Leslie, as they grew up.

Thank you for the way you have demonstrated, with your life, the love of God.

And thank you for the love and servant spirit you have shown to your family during these 55 years of marriage, and especially during the years I have been in a wheelchair.

Also, thank you for your help and patience in helping me to write this book.

Federal Judge Bill Osteen, Sr.
A Gentleman Giant

"He has showed you, O man, what is good; and what does the Lord require of you but to do justice, and to love kindness, and to walk humbly with your God."
Micah 6:9, KJV

William Lindsay (Bill) Osteen, Sr. was born at St. Leo's Hospital in Greensboro on July 15, 1930. His father was John Luke Osteen and his mother was Ruth Tatum Osteen. Bill had one brother, John Luke (Jack) Osteen, Jr., five and half years older than he.

In 1935, the Osteens moved to a 65-acre farm on Muirs Chapel Road, about six miles from downtown Greensboro. There was no electricity and no indoor plumbing. Their water came from a well, and the toilet was about 100 feet from the house.

Ruth, Bill's mom, was reared in Rowan County, North Carolina, and she was a woman with a deep faith in God. She was a good cook and loving mom, who was blessed with a beautiful singing voice and a talent for playing the piano. Because of his father's demanding work schedule, Bill's mom reared him and Jack almost by herself. Although the two boys probably deserved it, Ruth never spanked either one. She disciplined by example. Unfortunately, she died of cancer in 1953.

Bill's dad, John, was born in a log cabin in Osteen Cove in the mountains of western North Carolina. John graduated from Fruitland Institute and then, during the summers, he attended the University of North Carolina in Chapel Hill, North Carolina. He taught school for some time and then served as a principal. Later he worked for the United States Treasury Department in the Prohibition Administration Division during the time when liquor was outlawed, with assignments in Asheville, Charlotte, Salisbury, and finally, Greensboro. It was during these years that Bill's parents met, fell in love, and were married.

John Osteen became the first U.S. Probation Officer in the Middle District of North Carolina, where he served for three decades. From 1966 to 1968, he served as State Senator from Guilford and Randolph Counties. When Osteen died in 1980 at the age of 88, he was described as "a mountain man, but of a strong independent stock. He combined devotion to justice with a sense of compassion and humanity." He was a father who set an example of courage, character, and faith for his two sons, Bill and Jack.

Bill's brother, Jack, graduated from West Point Military Academy in 1948 and became a platoon leader in the Korean War in 1950. Jack survived that war and returned home to marry Pat Hannum in 1954. They have three children, Lindsay, Luke and Ann. When war broke out in Vietnam in 1968, Osteen returned to combat.

Major General John Luke (Jack) Osteen is now retired and lives with his family in Brevard, North Carolina.

Life on the farm was a wonderful experience for Bill and his family. Most of the farming was done by tenant farmers, while the Osteens cared for a large vegetable garden. They also had cows, horses, mules, and pigs to care for. Their two-bedroom home didn't have central heat, so Bill kept warm on cold winter nights by sharing his bed with his dog, "Tip". The heat and fuel for cooking was supplied by wood which Bill and Jack chopped. To take a bath, water had to be brought from the well and warmed on the wood stove.

When Bill was a young boy, he often would go out to the barn, climb up on a barrel, and preach to the horses, mules, goats, and pigs. Bill put God first in his life always. In later years, he considered the Christian ministry, and also medicine and law.

At the age of 14, Bill volunteered to play taps on his new trumpet for the Memorial Day service at Guilford High School where he attended. He did not hit a single note correctly, not surprising since he had not had a single trumpet lesson. He was very confident that he could handle the situation.

Athletics were a big part of his life. In high school, he played basketball, football, and baseball. Bill was extremely active in other school activities: president of the freshman class, Beta Club, Athletic Club, Student Council (president, one year), and the Teen Club. He was voted: Most Likely to Succeed, Most Tactful, Most Ambitious, Best Dressed, and Most Polite.

Guilford College was the next stop for young Bill Osteen. He played football, basketball, baseball, and golf for the college. A near tragic event occurred during this time. One of Osteen's college friends was taking flying lessons. He invited Bill and his girlfriend to join him and his girlfriend for an afternoon of flying. All went well until the new pilot decided to show off and took the plane down closer to the ground. As they descended, Bill saw the high tension wires in front of them and started to yell, but too late. The plane hit the wires, severing one wing and plunging to the ground upside down in a heap of metal. A telephone repair man showed up about twenty minutes after the crash. He helped Bill out of the plane, and the two of them pulled the other three out of the wreckage. Everyone in the plane was covered in gasoline, but miraculously, fire never erupted. The pilot suffered a broken back, but the others escaped with only cuts and bruises.

Bill later reflected, "You can't walk away from an experience like that and not ask who spared you and why you were spared." Of course, Bill knew the One who had saved him—both his life and his soul—and the record shows that he set about living up to God's purpose for "so great salvation" (Hebrews 2:3).

Bill was drafted into the army after his first year of college. Fortunately, he was honorably discharged with the rank of Sergeant and didn't have to go into combat in Korea.

After returning to Guilford College, Bill continued to play football, basketball, baseball, and golf, as well as doing well in the classroom. He graduated and enrolled in the Law School at the University of North Carolina.

After graduating from UNC Law School, Osteen moved to North Wilkesboro, North Carolina, to work with the Bill McElwee firm at a starting salary of $200 per month. Two years later, he moved back to Greensboro and started his law practice in the Jefferson Building. After about a year, Bill entered a practice with Roy Booth which later became Booth, Osteen, Adams, Fish and Upchurch with offices on Edgeworth Street.

Joanne Snow returned to Greensboro after graduating from Duke and was considering law as a profession, especially since her father was a lawyer. While she was working for the Adams, Kleemeier, Hagan, and Hannah Law Firm, Walter Hannah introduced Joanne to Bill Osteen. They started dating in October, 1958, were engaged by February, and married on May 16, 1959. On May 16, 2009, Bill and Joanne celebrated their 50th wedding anniversary.

Joanne grew up in Richmond, Virginia, the only child of John Edward (Jack) Snow and Dorothy Williams Bennett Snow. Her father practiced law with the firm of Pollard and Bagby. This was during the depression of the 1930's, and lack of business made it necessary for Jack to take another job with the Federal Reserve Bank where he stayed until 1953. It was then that Joanne's parents moved to Greensboro where her father became vice president of the Federal Home Loan Bank. Ultimately, he returned to his law practice. After 49 years of marriage, Joanne's father died of a heart attack in 1985 and her mother lived until 1999.

In March of 1960, Bill decided to run as a Republican for the North Carolina House of Representatives. No Republican had represented Guilford County in Raleigh for over fifty years, so this was a giant undertaking. Campaigning day and night with speeches, TV shows, and door-to-door visits, Bill won a very close race. Serving on 21 committees in the Legislature, Bill worked hard and won much respect from other Republicans and from Democrats as well. He won reelection in 1962 and was chosen Minority Leader of the House for both the 1961 and the 1963 sessions. After the 1963 session of the Legislature, Bill returned full-time to the law practice with Roy Booth, Pat Adams, Connie Fish, and Fred Upchurch.

While Bill was heavily involved in politics those four years, two sons were born, Bill, Jr. and John, with Bob being born later, in 1966. When Bill came home on weekends, he would spend Saturday mornings on the radio informing the public of the matters taken up in the legislature. After he would come home, he would pick up his golf clubs (He almost became a professional golfer before law school.) and head for the golf course. One Saturday, three-year-old Bill, Jr. asked, "Daddy, can't you stay home one Saturday?" Bill put the clubs down and did not play again for twenty years. This decision speaks volumes about the character and love of family of this great man.

In 1968, Bill ran for the United States House of Representatives against Democrat Richardson Preyer. It was a difficult campaign requiring long days of mailings, television, speeches, raising financial support, etc. Bill made a point of instructing all his supporters to treat opponents with the utmost kindness, even though he was not always treated that way. The election was extremely close, but Bill lost by only a very small percentage of the vote.

A few months later, President Richard Nixon appointed Osteen United States Attorney from 1969 until 1973. All reports are that Bill did an outstanding job as U.S. Attorney. He resigned in 1973 and joined with Pat Adams, Woody Tilley, and Ralph Walker in a law firm with offices in the BB&T building. In 1985, Bill, Jr. joined the firm, and the six years practicing law with his son were what Bill, Sr. terms his best years of practice. Their firm dealt primarily with criminal cases, but also included estate work, divorce representation, and other civil matters. Bill worked hard on every case, regardless of whether he was being paid well or not. He felt everyone had the right to have the best possible counsel.

A good description of Bill Osteen, Sr. is that he was a Christian gentleman who loved God, loved his church (Greensboro First Baptist), and loved his family. He was a loyal friend, great storyteller, and hard worker, who had respect for everyone, regardless of economics, race, or ability. In addition, he was also a scholar, an astute politician, a talented athlete, and a man of great personality and integrity.

President George H. W. Bush nominated Bill to become a Federal Judge for the middle district of North Carolina in the spring of 1991. Bill accepted this nomination, and the entire family went to Washington for his interview by the Senate Judiciary Committee. The appointment for judge was June 18, 1991, and the impressive swearing-in ceremony was September 17, 1991. It was a busy time for the Osteens because in addition to all the above, Bill and Joanne's son, Bill, Jr. married Elizabeth King Holt on July 21, 1991.

While serving as Federal Judge from 1991 to 2007, Bill had a variety of cases. The tobacco case was very high profile, and there were many others involving drug transactions. Anti-trust issues, illegal aliens, bank robberies, racketeering, extortion, bribery, and corruption. Throughout his sixteen years as a Federal Judge, Bill enjoyed a reputation for honesty, professionalism, and ethical conduct. He had an innate and keen sense of right and wrong. He always acted with diligence and competence. He was fair and judicious in his approach to all questions and eloquent in his expression of thought. As a U.S. District Judge, Bill was appropriately firm and authoritative, but also compassionate.

In a letter to President George W. Bush on September 14, 2007, Bill Osteen, Sr. announced his retirement as a Federal Judge. Shortly afterward, President Bush appointed Bill Osteen, Jr. to succeed his dad as the N.C.

middle district federal judge. This was the first time in the history of our country that a father-son presidential team appointed a father-son team to be judges in the federal court.

Bill and Joanne learned in 2004 that Bill was diagnosed with melanoma, a deadly type of cancer for which there is no known cure. Everyone who knew Bill knew that he was a fighter and that if anyone could beat this affliction, it would be him. So, Bill and Joanne visited different specialists not only in Greensboro, but in different cities. They tried different treatments for this disease, but nothing seemed to work. None of us knew how terrible the pain was at times, but we were aware of how courageously and graciously he endured the pain. Often he would insist on going with Joanne to be with family and friends when he really didn't feel well and the pain was intolerable. Bill was demonstrating how to handle adversity. He also was modeling what it meant to finish strong with what he had left.

Bill underwent three surgeries in 2004 and 2005, one more in 2006, and another in 2007. He had treatments done in the hyperbaric chamber in Greensboro plus experimental procedures with specialists in Charlotte. In addition, he had radiation and chemotherapy during 2007 and 2008 resulting in losing his hair on two different occasions.

Despite these medical treatments, Bill finished strong in many ways. He continued to serve as a Federal Judge from 2004 until September 14, 2007. Also, he was chairman of the Judges Codes of Conduct Committee from 2001 through 2004. This was a difficult job which required extensive travel and the addition of another fulltime law clerk to Judge Osteen's staff.

On one occasion in 2006, there was a need for a judge to go to Boise, Idaho to help relieve a case overload. Even though he had just been released from the hospital, Bill felt duty-bound to make the trip. He showed up for court with a tube protruding from his neck and bandages covering almost half his face. The report was that Judge Osteen did an admirable job handling the cases. A local physician removed the tube before he returned home to Greensboro.

In the spring of 2007, Bill and Joanne joined a group from First Baptist Church to travel to Israel. This was a strenuous trip requiring much walking, climbing, and standing. Even with his illness, Judge Osteen kept up with the group despite the fact that he could hardly move when he first got up in the morning

Their son, Bob, married Jennifer Justice in October of 2007 in a beautiful ceremony in Charleston, South Carolina. On the day of the wedding, Bill could hardly walk, but since he was the best man, he somehow summoned the strength to stand for a considerable length of time until the ceremony concluded.

These are just a few examples of the indomitable spirit of Bill Osteen. He refused to give up. He was determined to finish strong.

Through all theses struggles, Bill never lost his sense of humor, his love for people, his optimism, or his excitement for life. Many times in the last years, someone would ask Bill how he was doing. Usually he would politely ignore the question and ask them how they were doing, how is the family, or what's going on with your job.

Finally, after all known possibilities were exhausted for a cure for Bill, the melanoma cancer just kept advancing, and Bill grew weaker.

On August 9, 2009, Bill Osteen, Sr. passed away. After his death, a Celebration of Life service was held before a capacity crowd at the First Baptist Church. The following are some excerpts from a wonderful tribute to Bill by Dr. Steve Pressley on that occasion.

"On Sunday afternoon, a small radio played softly on the table back of Bill's bed. It was turned to a religious radio station and *The Lord's Prayer* was being sung: 'For thine is the kingdom, and the power, and the glory forever, Amen' were the words that accompanied his final breath."

"For a long time, he had known he was mortally ill and that he must decrease. The same did not hold for the Lord Jesus who he had worshipped and served for all of his years. As for the Lord, He—in the words of John the Baptist and in the mind of Bill Osteen—He must increase. The story of Bill Osteen is a story of the increase of Jesus Christ in one man's life, from the time of his first redemptive encounter to the moment the Lord leaned down and gathered his servant unto himself."

"During the years, Bill had a unique and natural way of being and remaining a man of God, even as he functioned as a man of the law."

"Bill understood that no final cure was possible in our present life—not for any of us. What he was contemplating was a solution far more extensive and durable. In John 3:14-15 (NIV), Jesus told Nicodemus, 'Just as Moses lifted up the snake in the desert, so the Son of Man must be lifted up, that everyone who believes in Him may have eternal life.' Even at his most painful times, Bill upheld quality and made quality possible for everybody around him. This was born, no doubt, of the deep respect he had always maintained for everyone, in every circumstance, all across his field of vision."

"Nevertheless, there came the time in the hospital when he mentioned that thing that few had the heart to mention to him: his approaching death."

"'Something I've been wanting to ask," he said, 'Is it all right to pray that you won't just linger and suffer, and create suffering for all of the people you love? Or is all of that something that we just have to leave to God?'"

"Well, that appeared worthy of investigation, so we sat and explored our mutual recollections of the way the Lord works in people's lives, and especially toward the end of their lives. Together we remembered that we had known people to die in different ways. Some from accidents, some from illness. And others owing to a sudden catastrophic event relating to their heads or their hearts. These, we agreed, seem the fortunate ones, at least in some ways."

"Whether the manner of any of these deaths was influenced by the prayer of the one dying is an open question. Most of us think we know how we would wish to die, but does God respond to that? There is a chapter in Proverbs that reminds us of what ought to be obvious— that all of us have a will and a way, but God remains in the driver's seat. 'The human mind plans the way,' we read, 'but the Lord directs the steps' (Proverbs 15:9, NRSV). David said it even better, 'My times are in Thy hand' (Psalm 31:15, KJV)."

"Still more of these recollections addressed the crux of the Judge's question. For what he essentially was asking was this: Is it all right to ask God for what you want? Well, is it all right for his children and grandchildren to ask him for what they wanted? No question about that, of course, and if Bill were able to grant what they wanted, he did."

"Asking and granting is the most fundamental element of human relating. It may, in fact, be also the most essential ingredient to our kinship with our Father in heaven. The Lord himself said, 'Ask, and it shall be given you; seek, and ye shall find; knock, and it shall be opened unto you' (Matthew 7:7, KJV)."

"If Bill were to have his wish about what you and I would carry away from the experience of this day, I am sure he would encourage us toward such asking, seeking, and knocking at God's door. Much more than a memory of himself, he would want us to open our hearts to the true worship of God, to the believing study of His Word, and to the living of lives of faith in everything that we do."

"What we observe—and to be sure—what we celebrate today is that Judge Bill Osteen has knocked, and the door at last has been opened. Yes, he has decreased. Over the last months and years we have witnessed that. But in ways too numerous to mention, and known by so many of us in this room, The Lord of his life and his love and all of his future has increased."

"On Bill Osteen's watch, Jesus Christ has increased. And that being so, for Bill—as for John the Baptist, who stood on the banks of the Jordan River and watched Jesus drawing near. . ."

"This joy of (his) is now complete."

One of the most prestigious of all legal awards is the Fourth Circuit Inns of Court Professionalism Award. Bill Osteen, Sr. received this award on June 26, 2009. His speech at that ceremony was the last time we were privileged to hear his gifted oration.

The following are excerpts from an eloquent tribute to his father delivered by Bill Osteen, Jr. on November 25, 2009. (This article, used with permission, was first published in the March/April, 2010 issue of *The Bencher*, a bimonthly publication of the American Inns of Court.)

"Whether personally or professionally, all who knew him were touched by Judge Osteen's life. He unfailingly placed others before himself. For some, the old saying

'God is first, my family and friends are second, and I am third' is nothing but a saying. But for Judge Osteen, it was a way of life, and he would not be happy with any profile that failed to mention that of which he was most proud, and to which he was devoted—his family—his wife of fifty years, Joanne, and their children and families: Bill, Jr., Elizabeth, Anne Bennett, Bill III, John, Bob, Jennifer and Chace. However, everyone who knew him, knew the same man of character, and the wisdom, integrity, devotion, love, and humor that those of us in the family saw every day."

"Speaking of his sense of humor, it was legendary. He could always get the last laugh, although always with a great spirit and never in a mean way. It would be impossible to fully share his sense of humor in this short tribute, but he did prompt a fond chuckle from all of us with the following he wrote in his will:

'Please remember that my joy came from my family and friends and cannot be added to by an extravagant funeral. I really want a simple box to be in for I will not be there very long. It might help if you pay the preacher and the singers pretty well for I do want God to know I am coming.'"

A Partial List of Honors and Awards for Judge William L. Osteen, Sr.

President of University of North Carolina Law School Association – 1955-1956
Alumni Council UNC Law School
Member, Board of Visitors of UNC Law School and Wake Forest University School of Law
Distinguished Alumni, Guilford College
President, Greensboro Bar Association – 1989-1990
Vice President, North Carolina Bar Association – 2005

Past Member, Federal Bar Association

Greensboro Zoning Commission

Greensboro Human Relations Commission

Fellow, American College of Trial Lawyers

Federal Judge's Code of Conduct Committee – 1995-2001; Chairman 2001-2004

Distinguished Service Award, Greensboro Bar Association – April 15, 2004

Outstanding Alumni of the Year, UNC Law School – October 13, 2008

John J. Parker Award – May, 2008

Fourth Circuit Inns of Court Professionalism Award – June 26, 2009

Greensboro City Council Resolution honoring the memory of Honorable

William Lindsay Osteen, Sr. – February 16, 2010

Dedicated Member of First Baptist Church, Greensboro—1995-2009

Lynda and Hurley Hinshaw
Serving God Together

"Happy are those who long to be just and good,
for they shall be completely satisfied."
Matthew 5:6, KJV

If you had an occasion to visit a nursing home or retirement community in the vicinity of Randleman, North Carolina, you might see an attractive lady entertaining the residents. She could be clogging, doing an imitation of Carol Burnett's cleaning woman routine, or she might be playing the pan. Playing the pan is a delightful display of using her fingers and elbow to coax rhythm sounds out of a common kitchen pan. This is accompanied by singing.

Lynda Hinshaw has other fun parts in her routine, and she does them all with energy, joy and talent. The elderly residents love her.

And she does this all despite being a victim of Parkinson's Disease for the past eight years. Just getting out of bed is an ordeal for Lynda. Before her daily medicine takes effect, she experiences an unbelievable weakness in her body and legs. Usually, she can hardly walk and she gets around with very short steps. Fortunately, her husband, Hurley, is always there to help out.

In addition to entertaining at the various retirement communities and nursing homes around Randleman, Lynda also belongs to a Parkinson's support group and she entertains them. She also performs for church functions and the Asheboro library. Unbelievably, Lynda still has enough energy to serve as secretary for the United Society of Friends Women. She also serves on the church hospitality committee and the nominating committee and attends Bible studies and other church functions.

Lynda has a special love and compassion for elderly people whom she visits regularly and puts a smile on their faces. She calls one elderly lady every day and spends time with her often.

Lynda said, "When I get out of bed each morning, I praise God that I can do what I do. I could easily become discouraged, but I try to think positive and stay cheerful."

Lynda's husband, Hurley, is a very interesting gentleman. He was brought up in a Christian home and since boyhood has been an active Christian with a strong faith in God.

Hurley plants a big garden each spring with a variety of vegetables and about 200 tomato plants. He *gives* these vegetables and tomatoes away. He will not accept money for the vegetables and for thousands of tomatoes he gives away.

He likes helping others by cutting wood for the elderly or disabled and cooking venison roasts and hams. Not only does he supply these things; Hurley will also deliver them.

Having been born on a family farm in Cedar Square, North Carolina, Hurley Hinshaw knows how to work hard. He and his two brothers and a sister milked cows, fed chickens, gathered eggs, took care of a big garden, and also helped with the housework. In addition, they walked a mile and a half to catch the school bus.

According to Hurley, "My faith in God has made me a stronger person, and He is first and foremost in my life." Over the years, he has served as Sunday School teacher, youth group leader, usher, and a member of the board of trustee, the cemetery committee, and the Quaker Men.

In 1997, Hurley was diagnosed with prostate cancer and had a radiation seed implant December 31. After being in remission for eleven years, the cancer resurfaced in 2008. In December, 2009, a procedure called cryosurgery was performed, but it was unsuccessful.

Hurley reports, "The cancer is still there, but I know that God is in control and only He knows what my future will be. I stay positive and upbeat and don't dwell on the negative side of things."

Hurley and Lynda were married in October of 1998. They both worked at Piedmont Natural Gas in Greensboro, North Carolina, and had known each other for years. Both had previous marriages. Hurley was married to his first wife for 34 years, before she died of breast cancer. They had one daughter and two grandchildren.

Lynda's first marriage lasted several years but ended because of irreconcilable differences. There were no children in this marriage.

A remarkable thing about this inspiring couple is the peace, joy and love they exhibit, despite the physical problems they both have, plus the numerous tragic incidences in their family. Both of Hurley's parents died of cancer at age 50. Also, his twin brother and wife both died of cancer when they were 53. Hurley's sister died in her sleep at age 54.

Lynda's family history included some sad times also. When she was nine years old, several of her family members were severely injured in an automobile accident. Lynda's oldest brother and father both committed suicide in later years. Later, her mother had two heart attacks but she survived these. In addition, Lynda had to deal with a broken marriage.

A wise man once said: "Death is universal; everyone dies, but not everyone lives." Hurley and Lynda Hinshaw are two people who are really living. Despite all the difficult things that have happened to them—despite cancer and Parkinson's, this special couple is finishing strong with what they have left.

This is a passage in the New Testament where Jesus was telling a parable about the man who had very few talents but he invested them well. The Hinshaws have certainly invested their talents well.

"His Lord said to him, 'Well done, good and faithful servant. Thou hast been faithful over a few things. I will make thee ruler over many things. Enter thou into the joy of my Lord.'" Matthew 25:33, KJV

Royce Reynolds

King of the Crowns

"I can do all things through Christ which
strengtheneth me."
Philippians 4:13, KJV

It was a desperate time for young Royce Reynolds. He was in his fourth summer selling Bibles and other Christian books for the Southwestern Company. Royce had done well in previous summers. This summer he was assigned a territory in Danville, Virginia. He was just out of the army and left for the field brimming with confidence. When he arrived in the book field this time, however, he realized that after three years away from selling, he had lost his touch. For two weeks, he had not sold one book. Since he was working on straight commissions, he had worked two weeks with no pay.

Royce had a wife back in Knoxville, Tennessee and debts to pay. Finally, exasperated with his failure, he stopped in the middle of the lonely, dusty road and knelt down on his knees and began to pray. He told the Lord he needed a spiritual partner. He promised the Lord that he would give him ten percent of his earnings that summer if he would help him make some sales.

Two days later, Royce really started selling. That summer he made $3750 net. When he got back to Knoxville, Royce walked in to see the minister at his church and wrote him a check for $375. When the minister asked if he could afford it, Royce replied, "You don't understand. I have to pay off my Partner. This is His share." That is how Royce's stewardship began.

Royce Reynolds was born into a farming family in Flat Creek, Tennessee, a rural community near Franklin, which is 20 miles south of Nashville in the rolling hills of middle Tennessee. Born February 16, 1932, Royce was the first of James and Florence Reynolds' three children. The Reynolds owned a 106-acre farm where they grew tobacco and also a large vegetable garden. Royce and his father milked a dozen cows twice a day. There were also sheep and other animals to care for, including a horse that he rode to school.

Florence Reynolds was an ambitious woman and better educated than Jim. In the years to come, she would pour her own unfulfilled ambition into her children, especially Royce. She told him over and over, "Get all the education you can, and make Christ the center of your life." Florence provided the children with a generous supply of books, even giving them as Christmas presents instead of toys.

After the farm work was done, books became both an adventure and an escape. Royce had a favorite spot to read under a tree on a hill that overlooked the farm.

Once he became aware there was a big world beyond the little farm where the family barely made ends meet, he was ready to leave and never come back. Books had become Royce's doorway to the world.

Florence Reynolds was the religious leader in the family. The children learned Bible stories and they all prayed before meals. She taught her children that God loved them and that He was the source of every good thing. She taught them to love God, to obey His commandments, and to give to Him the praise and thanks that He deserved.

When Royce was about eleven years of age, he joined the Boy Scouts. With much hard work and determination, he earned the prestigious Eagle award in three years. This award enhanced a growing sense of self-confidence.

Royce graduated from high school in 1949 at age 17. He was so eager to get away from the farm that he enrolled immediately at Middle Tennessee State Teachers College in Murfreesboro and started classes in the summer. He had a few hundred dollars that he had saved by working for his father and other farmers.

His father took him to catch the bus to Murfreesboro. He put Royce out at the bus stop and told him that from now on he was on his own. He had done all he could for his son. That suited Royce fine because he had no plans to ever return to the farm.

Reynolds immediately found part-time work to help pay for his college expenses. His earnings plus the money he had saved was enough to get him started. The next summer, Royce landed a door-to-door sales job selling Bibles and Christian books with the Southwestern Company. This was a very difficult job, but Royce developed into one of the best salesmen they had ever had. The first summer Royce made $1250 net after paying all his living expenses.

Selling books that summer did more than provide money Reynolds needed to stay in college. He was gaining a self-confidence he hadn't felt since he earned his Eagle award in the Boy Scouts. He soon realized that his ability to sell would open up opportunities that he had never known before. He also found out that talking to people about the Bible time after time each day strengthened his faith. The job became part of his faith experience. Royce wound up working six seasons at this job.

Shortly after graduating from college, Royce made one of the very best decisions of his life—he married Jane Warren. After his marriage, he served a tour of duty in Austria with the U. S. Army.

Once his enlistment was up, Royce and Jane moved to Knoxville, where Jane went to work with the telephone company and Royce enrolled at the University of Tennessee Business School. After graduate school, he began to think seriously about his business future.

He considered becoming a minister but finally decided that God was not calling him to this work. He also thought about working full-time for Southwestern, the book company. Then Royce heard about a wonderful opportunity to work for a Pontiac car dealership in Birmingham, Alabama. He was not excited abut the prospect of selling cars, but the owner told him he could wind up owning his own dealership. That closed the deal. This would turn out to be another very wise decision that Royce would make.

He rose rapidly up the ladder, first working as sales training manager, then as new car sales manager, and then becoming general sales manager. After this, Royce became general manager for the entire company and part owner.

During these years, Royce and Jane were blessed with the birth of Ingrid and Warren.

By the late 1960's, Royce's leadership in the Pontiac car dealership was making him rich. By the early 70's, Reynolds owned forty percent of the Pontiac dealership. In addition, he and a partner had opened a Pontiac store in St. Petersburg, Florida, in 1969. They also had equal shares in other Birmingham dealerships selling Mercedes-Benz, Volvo and Nissan.

Reynolds' decision to remain in the car business had paid off handsomely, but ambition still drove him. He wanted to own more dealerships, but his partner was satisfied with their present success. The existing businesses Royce owned were enough to provide financial security for the rest of his life, but Royce was driven to do all that he could do.

Early in 1973, Reynolds bought the Zane-Waters Pontiac dealership in Greensboro, North Carolina, and moved his family there. It was a small dealership in a small town, but he had achieved one of his goals—he now was his own boss with his own business. He named the business Crown Pontiac. There were bumps in the road, but Royce moved the business to a new building on Wendover Avenue, obtained the Honda franchise, and things really took off from there.

Reynolds' businesses just kept on growing. By the mid-1980's, Crown customers could buy their choice of cars made by Pontiac, BMW, Honda, Audi, Mitsubishi, Dodge, and Nissan. Royce soon acquired dealerships in Chapel Hill and Raleigh, North Carolina, as well as in Richmond and New Orleans. In addition, he was part owner of dealerships in St Petersburg, Florida and in Birmingham.

By the middle 1990's, Crown was one of the leading automobile sales operations in the Southeast with twelve dealerships selling fifteen brands. In the late 1990's,

Royce was in his late sixties and beginning to think about retirement.

Near the end of 1998, Reynolds sold the Crown dealerships to Asbury Company. After forty-three years, Royce Reynolds had spent a lifetime making money and now was entering into a new phase of his life. The rest of his life would be devoted to giving it away, which was quite a challenging project.

Someone has said that person's life can be
divided into four stages.

1. Struggle – You go through the hard years when you are trying to be successful.
2. Success – You have reached that point. With the right amount of focus and determination, most people today can reach a level of success.
3. Surrender – You become fully aligned with a higher purpose for your life by trusting God.
4. Significance – You use your knowledge, experience, and resources gained by success to help other people.

Most people don't go through the significance stage unless they have experienced surrender. If you set your sights on attaining surrender and make the decision that you are going to be a blessing to others, the rest will come naturally. True surrender comes when you give your life to Jesus and commit yourself to His teachings.

Royce Reynolds went through all these stages. He certainly had years of struggles. He surrendered himself to Christ on the dirt road in Virginia when he was selling Bibles, door to door. He became extremely successful and wealthy. Over the years, Royce began to go through the significance stage, but the best was yet to come.

Selling his huge company proved to be a traumatic time for Royce. For many years, he had poured all his energy, talent for selling, time and leadership into building his company. Now he had to decide what to do with the rest of his life. There was a period of idleness while he pondered the various options. There was also a time of sadness, boredom, and even depression as Royce adjusted to the idea of not being in control, no longer handling the challenges of running a large company, and changing his sense of identity. He was too young and energetic to just retire and go to his home at Grandfather Mountain or Florida and play golf every day.

Royce had done very well in his life so far, and he wanted to finish strong. He understood that finishing strong is a continuous process of becoming a better vessel for God's purposes.

All his life, Royce had been exposed to the Bible and its teachings. It started with his mother as she read Bible stories to her children. It continued as he attended the little country church with his family. All his adult life, the church and being a disciple for Christ had been important to Royce.

It was no surprise then when Royce decided that with the extra time he now had, he would devote the majority of his time serving God by helping to strengthen His church. Royce plunged into this with the same energy, enthusiasm and leadership that was required to build his successful car business.

Space will not allow a listing of all the positions Royce has held in his church and in the entire Methodist denomination. Many of the ideas which made his business successful are now being used by the church.

The sense of calling and commitment that Royce experienced while selling Bibles door to door is still real to him. It is obvious in the way he continues to serve the church today. Royce Reynolds' deep conviction for helping his church win disciples for Christ and his generous gift of both time and money truly make him one of Greensboro's most outstanding citizens.

A Partial List of Ministries Financially Supported by Royce and Jane Reynolds

<u>Greensboro Urban Ministry</u> – A one-million-dollar endowment for church programs

<u>West Market Street United Methodist Church</u> – One million dollars for renovations to the church, plus regular contributions

<u>Greensboro College</u> – A multi-million dollar gift to convert a former YMCA facility to a student center. Many other gifts for an ethics program and a chaplaincy

<u>Boy Scouts</u> - $700,000 to build a new Scout office building

<u>Salvation Army</u> – More than one million dollars to help build the new Center of Hope in Greensboro

<u>Duke University</u> - $1.2 million to endow the Royce and Jane Reynolds Chair of the E. Stanley Jones Professor of Evangelism in the Divinity School.

<u>Center for Creative Leadership in Greensboro</u> - Endowed the Royce and Jane Reynolds program in church leadership. This program helps to develop effective pastoral leaders. It is endowed with a five-million-dollar bequest. This will ensure that the program will continue to bring pastors together for training, counseling and growth. Reynolds' purpose in supporting the program is to help develop visionary leaders for the church who will do a better job of making disciples of Jesus Christ.

<u>Royce and Jane Reynolds Leadership Academy for Evangelism and Discipleship</u> – The Reynolds agreed

to underwrite this two-year program at a cost of over $300,000. Its purpose is "to develop leadership gifts to equip them to lead their congregation to intentionally reach unchurched people for Christ and nurture them into mature discipleship."

"We make a living by what we get,
but we make a life by what we give."
Winston Churchill

Foy Flowers

A man who walks by faith and not by sight

> "Therefore if any man be in Christ, he is a new
> creature: old things are passed away; behold,
> all things are become new."
> 2 Corinthians 5:17

In Greensboro, North Carolina, there is a very busy and dangerous intersection. It is where Westridge Road ends at Friendly Avenue, a six-lane thoroughfare. At this juncture there sits Friendly Avenue Baptist Church.

Foy Flowers, age 69, and his wife, Marie, live a short distance from this intersection. Most days of the week, Foy can be seen walking west on Friendly Avenue and crossing over that street to get to the church. There is a traffic light there, but the heavy traffic and the speeding vehicles make this one of the most dangerous intersections in town. Despite that, Foy gets across the street time after time without incident.

His ministry is to volunteer for a variety of jobs at the church or to help church members. Some of his jobs include: assembling playground equipment, helping to erect large tents for outside activities, mowing the lawn, repairing appliances, installing ceiling fans, and fixing all types of electrical and plumbing problems. In addition, Foy assembles and installs ham radio antennas and even helped build a 15-foot high living Christmas tree for his church.

A few years ago, there was a severe ice storm in Greensboro. Trees fell all over town and especially in the beautifully wooded area of west Greensboro where Foy lives. Streets and sidewalks were blocked, many people couldn't get their cars out of their driveways, and traffic was snarled all over town.

Foy and his son, Jonathan, age 25, loaded up two chainsaws in their truck and went to work. They trimmed tree limbs off the trees and cut everything up into short pieces and cleared many driveways and streets.

What should surprise and inspire you is this: <u>Foy Flowers</u> <u>is</u> <u>TOTALLY</u> <u>BLIND</u>! His condition is not one in which he sees silhouettes, images or light. <u>He</u> <u>cannot</u> <u>see</u> <u>anything</u>!

Foy has had a severe problem with congenital cataracts since early childhood. He had partial eyesight then, but it was obvious he would not be able to attend public school. He underwent ten eye operations as a young child and there was some improvement. His family arranged for him to enroll at a special school in Raleigh where he was taught the skills needed to live a productive life despite his disability. Foy started in this school at the kindergarten level and stayed for thirteen years.

In his first year, the main emphasis was on learning Braille. In the following years, he studied traditional school subjects, along with acquiring skills to help him cope as a blind person. Foy's family was very poor and couldn't supply him with spending money. At age 9, he was taught how to make mattresses and put cane on the seats and backs of chairs. The shop where this was done was a part of the school for the blind. His eyesight at this time was 20/200 (what normal eyes could see at 200 feet, Foy could see at 20 feet). So Foy developed some skills as a nine-year-old, and even with his limited eyesight, was able to earn spending money.

During the thirteen years Foy attended the school for the blind, he lived in a dormitory and ate in the school cafeteria. Fortunately for Foy, the teachers, administrators, counselors, and other employees at the school were Christians. He heard the Bible read and Jesus lifted up from morning until night. This had a great influence on young Foy, and at twelve years of age, he accepted Christ as his Savior.

During this experience, Foy prayed, "God, I have nothing to offer but me. I want to give me to you." Foy had previously believed in God, and as an eight-year-old, had often prayed for his alcoholic dad. But this experience at age twelve was a complete surrender to God. The years at the school were difficult, but Foy's faith in God helped him get through it.

When he was 21, Foy met and married Marie. She, too, had limited eyesight and attended the school for the blind in Raleigh. They have been married 48 years and are blessed with two children, Jonathan, 25, and Stacy, 26. Jonathan is single and works for the city of Greensboro in the water department. Stacy is married and has two children. Both Jonathan and Stacy had eye problems, but are doing well now.

Even though Flowers had limited eyesight in his early and middle adult years, he was able to hold down several jobs. He worked for the Industry for the Blind for several years, Bonitz Insulation for about seven years, and then Gilbarco for twenty-eight years. His years with Gilbarco were rewarding and productive. Unfortunately, in the later years with Gilbarco, Foy's eyesight became progressively worse.

Finally, at age 56, Foy could no longer see well enough to do his job, and he retired. In appreciation for the years of service, Gilbarco agreed to continue paying Foy and Marie's insurance payment until they were 65 years old. It was about this time when Flowers was advised by his local doctor to go to Duke Hospital and have surgery on his eyes. The operation was not successful and since that time, Foy has been totally blind.

When asked by a friend about his reaction to this development, Foy explained, "God did not cause this, but He allowed it to happen. I don't blame God, and I know He has a purpose for me. My job is to find out what His purpose is and to be submissive to His will."

It is obvious that Foy has certainly done that. Earlier we have listed some of the projects he has been involved in.

In all the years Foy has been a member of Friendly Avenue Baptist Church, he has consistently been an encourager. His personality is upbeat and positive. He has a great sense of humor and enjoys joking with friends about his blindness.

Gary Church is one of Foy's best friends. They often visit church prospects together. On one occasion, when Gary was driving the two of them to a prospect's home, Foy said, "We're going the wrong way."

Gary was amused at his blind friend's remark. "What do you mean, 'We're going the wrong way?'" Gary asked.

Foy replied, "Well, I know where that street is, and you have to cross some railroad tracks to get there. We haven't crossed over any railroad tracks, so we must be going the wrong way."

Gary realized that Foy was right and enjoyed telling the story to everyone about how this blind man was able to give him directions.

Gary and Foy also visit the local jail regularly. They talk to the inmates about the love of God, read the scriptures, and give a personal testimony regarding their faith in God.

Foy can be very firm with the prisoners or he can be very sympathetic and loving. Sometimes when he encounters an inmate who is negative or is having a "pity party", Foy will say to him, "I'm blind; now, what's your problem?" "For God hath not given us the spirit of fear; but of power, and of love, and of sound mind." 2 Timothy 1:7, KJV

On other occasions, he will address them like this: "I love you, and God loves you."

Once an inmate replied, "How can you love us? You don't even know us, and you can't see us."

Foy answered, "Jesus is in my heart and that enables me to love you."

Gary reported that when Foy said that, tears flowed from his sightless eyes. The inmates were touched by this and their attitudes softened. According to Gary, a couple of the prisoners were won to Christ that night.

Some principles that describe Foy's beliefs:

- God has allowed my blindness—He has a purpose for me.
- God has protected me all my life.
- My inspiration is Jesus.
- Play with the hand you are dealt.
- Blindness is a blessing to me.
- I'm glad God made me this way.

Surely Foy Flowers is an inspiring example of finishing strong with what he has left.

Al Lineberry, Sr.

Legendary Community Leader

"Heaviness in the heart of man maketh it stoop;
but a good word maketh it glad."
Proverbs 12:25, KJV

Albert S. Lineberry, 92, died Sunday, July 11, 2010, and Greensboro lost one of its most admired civic leaders. The funeral service was scheduled for the following Wednesday in the First Baptist Church sanctuary.

Pastor Dr. Ken Massey, visited with the Lineberry family to offer condolences and to discuss the funeral service. The family had prepared an obituary which included five single-spaced pages of accomplishments and awards. According to Al Lineberry, Jr., "We gave this obituary to Dr. Massey, and he carefully reviewed it. Then he asked whether or not we should mention the fact that Al, Sr. was a member of First Baptist Church for over 54 years."

The family had forgotten to mention this! But of all his accomplishments, those who knew Lineberry, Sr. said he was first and foremost a man of faith. "Everything started with his religious feelings and beliefs," Al Lineberry, Jr. said. "Everything was an offshoot of that, giving back for what he felt God had given him. "

Dr. Massey completed the reading of the five-page obituary and then declared to the Lineberry family, "I can't use all this in my message at the funeral service — it's too much!" Massey continued, "I'm going to tell about Al Lineberry, the man and how he loved God and the church." According to Lineberry, Jr., the message by Dr. Massey at the funeral service was one of the most wonderful and inspired tributes he had ever heard.

The First Baptist Church was packed with friends, relatives, and admirers who came to say goodbye to a truly great man.

Dr. Massey opened his remarks with this statement, "Deeper than our grief today is our profound sense of gratitude and respect for the life and work of Albert Shuler Lineberry, Sr. Our lives, our community, our state, and our world have been blessed by this man of faith who showed us the meaning of the biblical phrase, "'Whatever thy hand findeth to do, do it with all thy might.'"

Dr. Massey reminded everyone that Al Lineberry was shaped in the heat and pressure of the Great Depression. He was a pilot in the Great War. He was a member of the "greatest generation," who had a sense of duty and who made a huge impact on our country and world. Al liked this generational mantra: Anything worth starting is worth finishing, and anything worth doing is worth doing right. Dr. Massey added that the greatest generation gave us many exceptional examples of service, strength, success, courage, perseverance, philanthropy, and faith. Al

Lineberry, Sr. stood very tall in his generation and these virtues are his legacy.

Dr. Massey continues, "My usual task in a funeral service is to touch on a few highlights of a person's life and faith. So I have an unusual problem today. I brought a list of organizations, offices, positions, and awards that make up Al's resume. You see this catalog of commitment and find it hard to believe it represents the stewardship of one man in one lifetime."

"But as this man often intoned: 'Life is not how long you live; life is how well you live. Life is not how much you make; life is about how much you give.' And I think Al would add: 'Faithfulness isn't about the length of your biography, but the quality of it.' This resume isn't just long; it's deep."

"These words of Jesus Al believed not only in his head but with his life: 'To whom much has been given, much will be required; and from one to whom much has been entrusted, even more will be demanded.' Al has been an active leader at First Baptist Church for over 54 years. He taught a men's study class, worked on many committees, chaired the finance committee many times, and also served as deacon chairman. Al Lineberry has been a pillar of this church."

Dr. Massey continued, "Al wanted to share his faith and was a longtime supporter of the Bill Glass Evangelistic Association. He wanted everyone to know the Lord who had so blessed him. And yet when you survey his life, his primary testimony, his greatest witness about Christ was his work for the common good in God's world. Al loved his community and the many organizations that worked for the betterment of one world. But all this service came from his obedience to Christ."

Dr. Massey ended his tribute with this prayer: "Lord, we know that you made Al Lineberry into a person who reflected your image on earth; who gave us a glimpse of your will in our lives, and we are grateful. We know that he cannot be replaced in this church or community, so we ask that you raise up others among us who can follow his example of stewardship and service. Grant to us those who have gifts of humor and grace, faithfulness and energy. Bring to us leaders who have the some capacity for justice and honor. And please, O Lord, hold this family in the palm of your hand, especially Al's wife, Helen. Be merciful to her and strengthen her until she is reunited with Al around your table of celebration."

Al Lineberry was 18 years old when he decided to leave Memphis, Tennessee, and travel to Burlington, North Carolina. Times were tough in Memphis in 1936, and young Al thought that his chances for a good job and success could be found in North Carolina.

Two of his father's married sisters lived in Burlington. They convinced Al to come to their town and were very helpful in assisting him to get a start there.

Before leaving Memphis, his work career consisted of working in an ice cream shop, as a golf caddy, and as an ice delivery man. After graduating from high school, Al worked in a bakery for $14 a week. He also worked as a carhop for $16 a week. Al was convinced there were better opportunities in North Carolina.

While driving with his uncle in North Burlington one day, they passed by the town funeral home, Rich and Thompson. As they drove past that funeral home, God spoke to Al in a very clear way. God told Al that the funeral business was what He wanted Al to get into. He had a difficult time sleeping that night, but when he awoke the next morning, the message was still clear. Lineberry told his aunt and uncle that he was going to apply for a job at the funeral home.

Strengthened by the belief that God was on his side, Lineberry confidently walked into the funeral home and asked for a job. The owner, Ernest Thompson, told Al he could spend his nights at the funeral home without pay. The position would also involve helping with emergency ambulance trips and answering the telephone.

Lineberry accepted the offer and spent three months working nights with no pay. He impressed the owners during this time and was given a fulltime job at a salary of $15 a month. Al made four times that at the Memphis bakery, but it was an enjoyable job that gave him a start in the business he would work at for a lifetime.

After more than three and a half years at Rich and Thompson, first as an unpaid trainee, then as an apprentice, and eventually as a regular employee, Al's salary climbed from $15 to $55 a month. It was at this time that he informed Ernest Thompson that he was resigning his job so that he could enroll in mortuary school.

Lineberry had no money saved but he was able to get three small loans. "It was almost as if God was opening a new door every time I faced a closed door and needed help," Lineberry said.

In the fall of 1940, Lineberry headed for mortuary school in Nashville, Tennessee. He worked as a short order cook to help with expenses, and in one year, had earned a degree from the College of Mortuary Science.

Al's first job out of school was with Lewis Funeral Home in Asheville, North Carolina. This was Al's first permanent job, with a starting income of $120 a month. He was on his way to becoming a funeral director.

Only a year after starting his new job, he volunteered for the U.S. Army Air Corps on November 10, 1942. This was almost a year after the Japanese attacked Pearl Harbor.

In addition to his job and the war, Lineberry met and fell in love with Helen Howerton. She was the daughter of one of Asheville's leading businessmen. Lineberry asked Helen to marry him soon after they met and she accepted. Despite delays in the wedding date imposed by her father, they were finally married on December 26, 1942. The wedding took place over two months before he was called to active duty. This proved to be a wonderful marriage that would last 67 years.

Al was called to active duty in February, 1943. He left his new bride behind with her parents. His first flight training took place in Miami, Florida. After a few other stops, he finally was assigned to Moody Field in Augusta, Georgia, where he was awarded his wings for flying. After all that training, Al was never involved in actual combat. When he arrived in Europe, the war there was ending.

Lineberry was discharged in October of 1945 with the rank of lieutenant. He came home to his wife and a new baby daughter who was born five months earlier while he was in England.

Now that his military service was over, Lineberry returned to work with Lewis Funeral Home in Asheville where his first son, Al Lineberry was born on October 1, 1946. In 1950, they had their third child, Patricia, and another son, Thomas, was born in 1954.

During these years, Al began to enter the social and civic scene and to renew his involvement with the church. It was during this time that Al's faith in God grew substantially. Two of his mentors were Reverend Perry Crouch and a young Baptist evangelist named Billy Graham.

By this time, Lineberry had left Lewis Funeral Home to work with a competing funeral home in Asheville. As his career progressed, he was able to acquire a minority share of Morris and Black Funeral Home.

In the spring of 1955, Lineberry negotiated a deal to purchase 51 percent ownership of the Hanes Funeral Home in Greensboro, North Carolina. A major problem was that he had no money to pay for half the business. The sellers worked out a payment schedule and no upfront cash was needed.

Lineberry drove back to Asheville and broke the news to his family. He then went to see his spiritual mentor, Reverend Perry Crouch. They prayed, asking God if this was the right thing to do. Their wives and children also prayed and asked for divine guidance. The family and the minister all agreed the move was the right one, and that faith and trust in God would see them through. So, the Lineberry family, which included four children and a pregnant wife, packed up and moved to Greensboro in October, 1955.

It was very difficult financially in the early years in Greensboro. Having to make the large monthly payment to purchase the business, along with meeting the payroll and paying all the other expenses involved with running the business was not easy. Al worked very hard. The business prospered and he took care of his financial commitments. It took years, but he finally paid off the Hanes and was also able to buy the remaining stock owned by others. This gave Al total ownership of the company. He changed the name of the business to Hanes-Lineberry and initiated a new marketing strategy. He began advertising on TV, a new tactic for funeral homes. Just as he had done in Asheville, Al became very involved in church and civic affairs in Greensboro. He soon became very well-known and highly respected for his selfless work in the community.

There were doubts in the early days that the business would survive, mainly because of a financial challenge inherited from the previous owners. God answered prayers and the funeral home began handling more services than ever before. Lineberry conducted regular prayer services at the funeral home for his staff and sometimes invited local ministers to lead the service.

In spite of the early business difficulties, Lineberry eventually became one of the city's most important leaders. In 1980, a poll of 580 local leaders voted Lineberry the second most influential and persuasive person in Greensboro. Only Mayor Jim Melvin finished ahead of Lineberry in the voting.

Lineberry also established himself as a leader among the nation's morticians. He was elected president of the National Selected Morticians in 1962.

Because of Lineberry's leadership, Hanes-Lineberry grew to become the third largest funeral service in North Carolina. He opened a second location near the coliseum and later purchased the Westminster Gardens cemetery in northwest Greensboro.

In 1990, the Lineberry family sold the business to a large conglomerate headed by Ray Loewen, a Canadian entrepreneur. Al Lineberry, Jr. formed a subsidiary of the parent company and named it The Lineberry Group. A third new Hanes-Lineberry facility was opened on High Point Road. Lineberry. Jr. sold the Lineberry Group back to The Loewen Group in 1997. Loewen eventually filed for Chapter 11 bankruptcy in early 2000. In a major reorganization of The Loewen Group, a new company was formed named The Alderwoods Group. Hanes-Lineberry became a part of Alderwoods in the takeover. As part of a large restructuring of funeral services, Alderwoods was later merged with Service Corporation International, the nation's largest funeral service company. Hanes-Lineberry is now in the top five percent of Alderwoods' funeral homes in size and service.

Even though his business required a lot of effort, Lineberry continued to devote much time and energy to his church and community. He had boundless energy and only needed about four hours sleep per night. He was a leader in the YMCA for over 60 years. He was active with the Boy Scouts, the local school board, and the Greensboro Chamber of Commerce. Lineberry was president of the Chamber in 1969 and helped to make this organization a leader in race relations and social advancement.

The next important job Al tackled was chairman of the school board. This came at a crucial time in Greensboro's history as it faced the need to desegregate its schools. His leadership in this role was marked by his integrity and fairness.

After leaving the school board responsibility, Lineberry took on other school and civic projects. During the late 70's and early 80's, he led campaigns to expand the YMCA and the Boy Scouts. He represented the Scouts in a meeting with President Jimmy Carter. Another important job came about when the American Baptist Association selected Lineberry and his wife, Helen, as delegates to go on a peace mission to Russia and neighboring territories.

In 1982, leaders of the Democratic Party asked Al to be their candidate for the U.S. Congress, in the Sixth District. The opponent would be Republican Eugene Johnston. Lineberry considered this opportunity and prayed about it as he traveled to Texas to take part in a Bill Glass Evangelistic Crusade.

He had finally decided to run for the office, but on the return flight to Greensboro, Lineberry suffered severe chest pain. A physician on the plane examined him and advised that he see a doctor as soon as he arrived back home. Unfortunately, a physical exam revealed that Lineberry had suffered a mild heart attack. The scare was enough to cause Al to cancel any plans to run for Congress that year. Robin Britt was chosen to run when Al dropped out, and he won the seat with Al's enthusiastic support.

Two years later in 1984, with his health improved, Lineberry easily won a seat in the N.C. House of Representatives. He served in this capacity for eight years. He was trusted and well-respected by the other lawmakers and was an effective representative for the people in his district.

The heart attack in 1982 was the first of several serious health issues for Lineberry. A few years later, he was diagnosed with cancer in his liver. This cancer was successfully removed by an operation. Then Al suffered his second heart attack. A pacemaker was implanted, and Al was soon gaining strength.

He was bothered at times by periods of depression but was still able to work in the family business and serve in the community. Al Lineberry, Jr. had been active in Hanes-Lineberry for several years, and he continued to take on more and more responsibility during these difficult years.

During this challenging time, Lineberry, Sr. served in the N.C. House of Representatives for eight years. He maintained a reduced but active role at Hanes-Lineberry, and he served as counselor and mentor to many. Lineberry helped with several fundraisers, worked with the Bill Glass Crusades, and continued his involvement with the Boy Scouts. He kept giving back to the community until 1997. The term, *"finishing strong"*, does not adequately describe this man's life.

Then, on April 15, 2002, a sad thing happened in the Lineberry family. Helen Lineberry, Al's wife, suffered a mild stroke. She was rushed to the emergency room at Moses Cone Hospital. The doctors there confirmed the stroke and kept her overnight for further tests. The next morning she was taken to the X-ray department. During the X-ray procedure, Helen was doing fine when, without warning, a paralyzing stroke engulfed her. She went limp, she couldn't talk, and she didn't even know her own name. The stroke wasn't fatal, but Helen was permanently changed. With therapy and time, her condition improved, and she has continued to be an inspiration to the whole family.

After Helen's strokes, Al, Sr. felt that God had called him to take care of her. He cut back on most of his business and civic responsibilities so he could spend more time with her.

Lineberry, Sr.'s philosophy on faith was that we should pray daily, worship regularly, witness with enthusiasm, serve sacrificially, and give generously. His mentor, Rev. Perry Crouch said this: "Much of what people accomplish in life, in business, and in civic affairs is often forgotten. But what you do for your church will live long after you."

Lineberry, Sr.'s top priorities were always his faith and his family. The way he lived his life proved this to be true.

Bob Romano and June Simpson

Leaders of "Helping Amputees Help Amputees"

"Pleasant words are as a honeycomb,
sweet to the soul and health to the bones."
Proverbs 16:24, KJV

Three to four times weekly, Bob Romano strolls into his place of ministry, the workout room at Spears YMCA in Greensboro, North Carolina. As he walks in, it's obvious that he has a slight limp. A closer look reveals that he is an amputee. One leg is normal, but the other leg has been amputated above the knee. Yet Bob walks quite naturally with the help of prosthesis.

There is usually a big smile on Bob's face as he stops at various work stations and talks with those who are exercising. His manner is upbeat and positive, and his words are encouraging. He never allows his conversation to drift into critical or negative areas.

Bob works out on the equipment himself, but he continually moves about the large room, spreading words of cheer and encouragement. His presence in that room is like a ray of sunshine.

In addition to the great work he does at the "Y", Romano is also president of "Helping Amputees Help Amputees" (HA-HA). June Simpson serves as secretary/treasurer of the organization. She too is an amputee, and she visits new amputees with Bob. When they visit amputees, their advice is, "Don't give up! You may have been dealt a bad hand, but play the hand you have. There are people to support you."

The amputee support group was founded in 2000 by Romano and other amputees with the support of the Moses Cone Health System. Robin Waldron, a physical therapist at Cone Outpatient Rehabilitation Center, was also helpful in starting the group.

Romano has faith in God and believes that God gives life its meaning and purpose. He also believes in heaven and believes that the things he is now doing help make his life worthwhile.

Bob and his wife have been married 56 years and have six boys and eight grandchildren.

Romano became an amputee in 1998. He and his wife were on vacation when another car crossed the center line and hit their car head-on. Injuries included a crushed knee and a compound fracture on his right arm, and both of his arms were cut open from his wrist and up past his elbow. His wife suffered severe injuries to her feet and knees.

Doctors at Pitt Memorial Hospital in Greenville, North Carolina, tried to save his leg, but they had to amputate his right leg above the knee. Romano said, "When you lose a limb, it's like grieving the loss of a loved one." He learned from experience the importance of support from other amputees as well as from his wife and family.

June Simpson's right hip was amputated in 1989 because of an infection resulting from a car accident. A total hip implant was broken and replaced. When she was only ten years old, June had osteomyelitis (bone infection in her right hip and left knee) which was almost fatal. There were years of surgeries to correct the deformities caused by the infection.

June went through a period of sadness and depression until she began reading a book about prayer by Catherine Marshall. Marshall discussed the importance of "claiming prayer", so June decided to pray this "claiming prayer", and it changed her life. She said, "A sense of peace came over me, and I knew that whatever happened, I would be all right."

When her doctor said her leg needed to be amputated at the hip, Simpson first hesitated, but later decided she would be better off letting the leg go. Eight months later, June really surprised her doctor when she walked into his office wearing a prosthetic leg.

Part of the wonderful ministry that Bob and June are involved with includes working closely with all the local hospitals in visiting amputees being treated there. They answer questions the amputees might have and discuss with them how they are living full lives in spite of being amputees.

Sometimes people who lose a limb are devastated and depressed. They feel like life is over, but that is not true. It is very encouraging for these new amputees to talk with Bob and June and see how full of joy their lives are, even though they have both lost a limb.

The mission of the support group led by Bob and June is to ensure that all amputees and the friends and families of amputees have access to information and support as they learn how to cope with limb loss.

This world is a better place because Bob Romano and June Simpson have been here. At an age when many people coast for the rest of their lives, Bob and June have chosen to give back and make a difference. They are both determined to finish strong with what they have left.

The Liz Dawkins Story
Everyone's Friend

"Encourage one another, and so much the more
as you see the day approaching."
Hebrews 10:25, KJV

Liz Dawkins is a lively, petite lady. She has a warm smile and a friendly demeanor. You get so engrossed in talking with her that you really don't notice the wheelchair.

She is fifty-one years old and she has depended on the wheelchair for over thirty years.

Liz was reared in a loving Christian home in Mayodan, North Carolina. She became a Christian as a young child. Her childhood was fairly normal until she was about seven years old. It was then that she began to suffer with nausea and balance problems.

Adding to her difficulties, Liz's brother was killed in a tragic automobile accident when she was ten years old.

This was a traumatic experience for Liz and the whole family.

After visiting different doctors, she was finally found to have a tumor on her brain. It was decided that Liz needed to undergo radiation treatments in order to kill the tumor. The radiation worked, but there were some negative side effects.

Liz was not able to go to school for several years, but she was home schooled and with hard work, she graduated from high school with her class. Later, Liz attended Rockingham Community College where she majored in business.

Because of her disabilities, Liz was not able to hold down a job for long. She found her niche, however, by serving as a volunteer teacher in a grammar school. Governor Jim Hunt presented Liz with a special award for volunteer service. This was a highlight for her.

She lives independently in Greensboro, North Carolina, accompanied by her pet parrot. Liz visits Spears YMCA at least twice per week. She is well-known there and has many friends. She stays healthy by exercising on several of the machines.

But just as important, Liz spreads joy and good cheer with everyone she sees. She likes to tell people, "Whatever doesn't kill you makes you stronger." Yes, Liz is finishing strong with what she has left.

The Clayton Story
Finishing Strong—My Story

"Let us run with patience the particular race
that God has set before us."
Hebrews 12:1, TLB

The pain in my lower back began early in the summer of 1990. At that time the discomfort was off and on and was usually helped by taking a couple of Advil tablets. As time went by, this pain became more severe and more frequent. Finally, in January 16, 1997, at the age of 63, I decided it was time for professional help.

I made an appointment with Dr. Sam Sue, a highly respected orthopedic surgeon in Greensboro. He ran a series of tests including an MRI. The MRI revealed the presence of a tumor inside my spinal column, at about belt level. Dr. Sue advised me to make an appointment with Dr. David Kelly, a neurosurgeon at Baptist Hospital in Winston Salem, North Carolina. After additional tests,

Dr. Kelly determined there was indeed a non-cancerous but aggressive tumor inside my spinal column. He recommended surgery as soon as possible because the tumor was advancing upward, and if not stopped, would cause considerable problems. Dr. Kelly also advised me of the dangers of this operation because of the presence of nerves in the same location as the tumor. After much prayer and discussion with my wife, Raydean, we decided to proceed with the operation.

On January 27, 1997, Dr. Kelly performed the procedure and declared it to be successful. After a time of healing, my life returned to normal with no immediate negative effects from the surgery.

Less than two years later, the tumor reappeared and during the last half of 1998, the pain grew progressively worse. On some days, I took as many as fifteen Advil tablets to get relief. It took some time spent in prayer, but I finally realized that God knows my needs infinitely better than I know them. And He is dependable, no matter which direction my circumstances take me.

Dr. Kelly operated again on February 25, 1999 and removed as much as possible of the new growth. Before the operation, he warned me again of the danger of nerve damage and also the peril of ignoring the problem. We again, after much prayer, gave him permission to proceed. The results of the surgery were not good. When I came out of the anesthesia, there was numbness in both legs and feet that I had not had before. I could move them and I could walk, but something was wrong.

In order to kill what was left of the tumor, I had radiation treatments for six weeks at Moses Cone Hospital. The radiation did not stop the tumor from growing. Desperate for a solution to this aggressive tumor, I visited specialists at Duke Hospital in Durham and M. D. Anderson Hospital in Houston, Texas. The doctors at these two locations agreed that I should begin treatment with an oral chemotherapy drug called Temodor. I started this treatment December 28, 2001 and ended it in May of 2004. In addition, I was a patient of Dr. Peter Enever at the Cancer Center at Wesley Long Hospital in Greensboro. He tried other types of chemo until finally the tumor growth stopped in the spring of 2005.

Starting with the operation in February, 1999, my legs grew progressively weaker. In addition to the medical treatments described earlier, I was involved in rigorous therapy sessions plus regular workouts in the fitness center at Greensboro Country Club. I was in a battle trying to build strength in my legs at the same time the nerve damage was causing my legs to get weaker. Also, I continued to play tennis at least three times weekly until I couldn't play anymore. My legs had gotten so weak that I began falling down on a regular basis, especially when playing tennis. Reluctantly, I had to stop playing a sport that I had thoroughly enjoyed for over 36 years.

During this six-year period, I went from a limp to a walking cane, then a walker, and finally, a wheelchair.

I'll never forget the day I finally stopped walking. It was January 5, 2006, and I was at a therapy session on Elam Avenue across the street from Wesley Long Hospital. Only two days earlier I was able to stand (with a little help from my physical therapist) and using my walker, cross the room—a distance of about fifteen feet. But on this day, I could not stand at all. I couldn't understand how my strength had diminished that much in just two days. Even though I knew my legs had been getting weaker and weaker over a considerable length of time, it still was an enormous shock to me that I could no longer stand or walk, even with the help of a walker.

Since I knew that the time when I would not be able to walk was drawing near, I had already purchased a wheelchair and a Dodge Van with a ramp and hand controls for acceleration and brakes. The chair was delivered on January 5, 2006. About the same time, I had a ramp built which would allow me to enter and exit our home.

The days following were a low time in my life. It was a time of depression and anger, targeted at my physician, at the radiologist, and at God Himself.

I had always been regarded as an optimist, but I certainly wasn't very positive during this period of time. I couldn't read the Bible; I couldn't pray; all I could do was feel sorry for myself. I was so frustrated! I called out to God, "Why did you let this happen? Why have you abandoned me? Why must I suffer this loss? Why do you not care?" I had always been an overcomer, but now I was overcome by depression and negativity.

When I lost the ability to walk, it was like going through a period of grief when a loved one dies.

Gradually, I began to come out of this negative fog. I'm grateful to my wife, Raydean, whose love and patience was greatly tested in those days.

During those long boring days in the hospital after my second operation in 1999, my thoughts would often go back to earlier years in my life.

I remembered that day when I was six years old, and we lived in Birmingham, Alabama. It was 1940, the Great Depression, and times were hard and jobs were scarce. My father, Roy, didn't have a job and my mom stayed home to care for my sister, Joyce, age 8, my brother, Buddy, age 4, and me.

One day our dad announced to us that he couldn't find a job anywhere in Birmingham. Therefore he had decided he was going to take a trip to Chattanooga, Tennessee to try his luck. Someone told him that jobs were available there. The next day, we all went down to the Greyhound bus station to see Dad off. We waved goodbye, not realizing that it would be twenty years before we would hear from him or see him again.

Mom tried unsuccessfully to contact him, but finally stopped trying. He never wrote or phoned us, and never sent money to help us survive.

This was devastating for Mom because she hadn't worked in years due to her responsibilities at home. She had no job, very little money saved, and three children depending on her. I truly do not know how she made it during those first weeks after Dad disappeared. I do know she spent a lot of time reading the Bible and praying.

The only solution she could come up with was to put the three of us into the Civitan Orphans' Home in Birmingham. My memories of the home are positive. They treated us well and fed us better than what we had been accustomed to. The biggest problem was that all three of us lived in different buildings for almost two years. Mom visited regularly and we talked about how it would be to live together again as a family. These were very difficult times for Mom, being away from her children, and adjusting to the reality of having been abandoned by her husband. She worked very hard at two jobs and lived frugally, saving all she could so she could afford to take us out of the Orphans' Home as soon as possible. Her faith, hard work, and resilience were instrumental in shaping my outlook and approach toward life.

That day finally came and it was a joyous time for the Claytons. We moved to a small house in the country near Rome, Georgia. Mom was able to get a job in a cotton mill there, and her mom moved in with us so that she could cook, clean and take care of us while Mom worked.

In 1944, the year I was ten years old, Mom married Bunk Culver, and we moved to Newnan, Georgia. A year later, I joined the Boy Scouts and met Scoutmaster Dewey Ward. I loved everything about the Boy Scouts and started advancing rapidly from Tenderfoot and on to the higher ranks. Dewey Ward took a special interest in me and encouraged me to do my best. This was the first time an adult other than Mom had ever really given me special attention and bragged on my accomplishments, and it filled me with self-confidence. At age 14, I was awarded the Eagle Badge. A newspaper article in the Newnan Times-Herald stated that I was the youngest Boy Scout in the history of our county to have earned this award. It also stated that only about one Boy Scout in a thousand earns the Eagle badge. My mom was asked to pin the Eagle on my shirt on the stage of the Town Hall in front of a large crowd. She was very proud of me and unashamedly cried in front of all those people.

Growing up in Newnan, Georgia was a wonderful experience. It was and still is a beautiful little southern town with a courthouse and town square. In those days, Newnan had the reputation of being the third richest town per capita in the country. The money came from textiles, peaches, and quite a few families who bought stock in Coca-Cola in the early days of its growth. There were many wealthy and outright rich families in Newnan.

Being exposed to the good life convinced me that I didn't want to remain poor the rest of my life. I worked hard in school and made good grades. Almost all my friends were planning to go to college, so about the eighth grade, I decided to attend Georgia Tech in Atlanta. They had a great reputation as an engineering school and engineers made good salaries, so that appealed to me.

One problem was that they wouldn't accept anyone unless they had an "A" average in high school. So I had to work hard to qualify for admission, and I made it. With the confidence I gained by becoming an Eagle Scout, I was pleased but not surprised that I was accepted at Georgia Tech.

My next hurdle was finding the $3000 it would take for the first year's expenses. My mom cleaned out her savings account and gave me $300. I headed to Atlanta on a Greyhound bus in the fall of 1952 with Mom's $300 and one cardboard suitcase. I knew I could find a part-time job around campus because I had been earning money since I was 10 years old. My best job was selling ice cream from a push cart the summer I was ten. I was paid a 10% commission on my sales and made as much as $40 per week. That was a lot of money in 1944, and most of it was turned over to Mom to help with family expenses. My brother and sister also worked and helped with the bills. Over the years, I also had jobs cutting grass, working in a drugstore and a jewelry store, doing road construction, and installing telephone poles. Our family had learned we all had to work hard even as children; we had to contribute most of our earnings toward family expenses. We all knew we had to trust God.

My first job in college was selling programs at the football games. I made it through the first quarter of my freshman year financially, but couldn't enroll for the second quarter starting in January because I was broke. I dropped out of school, worked full-time at a cotton mill in Newnan for three months, and when the third quarter started in April, I had the money to enroll. My favorite Bible verse then was "I can do all things through Christ who strengthens me" (Philippians 4:13, TLB).

I was able to win a $500 yearly scholarship my second year at Tech because of my grades. With that help and my part-time income, I was able to complete school with no more help from Mom and no student loans. Some of my jobs were dormitory advisor, feature editor of the school paper, and chemistry lab assistant. I graduated with a degree in Textile Engineering in the spring of 1957, the first member of my family to graduate from college.

My mom was a wonderful model for us in more ways than just with her work ethic. She taught us to read the Bible and to pray regularly. She took us to Sunday School and church almost every Sunday.

I was saved at age 13 during a revival at Oaklawn Baptist Church in Newnan. The baptism took place in a local lake. During the years that followed, I was active in church during high school and also at Georgia Tech, where I attended the First Baptist Church and was active at the Baptist Student Union.

God blessed me all through the years at Georgia Tech but especially during the spring of 1955. It was my third year in college, and I was returning to school to start the spring quarter. My transportation to Atlanta was a Greyhound bus. It was on this trip that I met Raydean Seckinger, a student nurse at Crawford Long Hospital in Atlanta. Little did I know this woman would become my wife.

Raydean told me a few months later that when she first saw me, God spoke to her in an inaudible voice, "That's the man you're going to marry." Then she thought, "That's the craziest thought I've ever had." Raydean was virtually engaged to a jet pilot and I was dating someone else. Also, we both had a long road ahead of us before graduation. She was one of the prettiest and most charming girls I had ever met. We had a lot in common, too. She was a Christian, she was deserted by her father when she was two, and her mother worked in a cotton mill to provide for four children. Raydean's love, faith, and support have inspired me in the good times and seen me through the bad. She has been a gift from God to me.

Thirteen months after we met on the Greyhound bus, we were married on April 21, 1956 at the First Methodist

Church in Atlanta. It was a simple but meaningful ceremony with just a few friends and family present.

In December of 1956, having successfully finished all requirements at Tech (I received my diploma in the spring of 1957), we moved to Greenville, South Carolina, where I began work at Deering-Milliken Company, a large textile mill chain. Raydean transferred her nursing credits to Greenville Hospital and continued her studies there. Three years later, I accepted a job with Blue Bell, Inc., a garment manufacturing company best known as the makers of Wrangler Jeans (V. F. Corporation). We moved to Mount Vernon, New York, a suburb of New York City, to begin my new job in sales, covering the states of New York and Vermont.

Our son, Alan, was born during the time we were living in Mount Vernon, on July 12, 1959. In order for me to be more centrally located in my sales territory, Blue Bell moved us to Syracuse, New York in 1960. It was in Syracuse that we were blessed with our second child. We adopted a beautiful little girl, three months old, whom we named Leslie. She was born on June 26, 1961.

Our next move was to Atlanta in 1962, where I had sales responsibility for the states of Georgia and Florida. My final move with Blue Bell was in 1964 when I was promoted to merchandise manager and assigned to the company headquarters in Greensboro.

During those years following, I earned an MBA (Masters in Business Administration) from the University of North Carolina at Greensboro. At age 35 and armed with an engineering degree from Georgia Tech, an MBA from the University of North Carolina at Greensboro, thirteen years work experience, and an unwavering faith in God, I was ready for the challenges ahead.

I left Blue Bell in 1969 and opened a retail business selling fabrics to those who sewed garments at home. This location was on South Davie Street on property now occupied by the Greensboro News-record. In 1971, we moved this store to a larger space at Quaker Village Shopping Center near Guilford College. The business grew at this location, especially after we expanded the scope of our business. We changed our name from Buttons and Bows to Clayton's Interiors in 1975. A second location on High Point Road was opened that year, and in 1976, we opened the third store in Friendly Shopping Center at the Forum Six Mall.

During the time all that was happening, in 1972, I bought a partnership in an old established company, Kinney-Keesee Office Furniture and Supplies (changed to Kinney-Clayton, Inc.). This company had two locations in Greensboro and one in Mount Airy, North Carolina. There were twenty-five employees doing a thriving business. A highlight with this company was a sale I made to the Melvin Municipal Building and the new courthouse. It amounted to twenty-six eighteen-wheeler trucks full of office furniture and equipment.

In 1973, two other men and I started a real estate investment company. Our mission was to buy and rent residential homes and apartment buildings. We were successful in buying quite a few properties, mostly with borrowed money.

The rapid growth of my different enterprises took its toll on me and my family. Not only was I involved in all these business, I also had several jobs at Lawndale Baptist Church, including Chairman of Deacons and Chairman of the Finance Committee, Men's Ministry Leader, R.A. Leader, and adult teacher. There were too many 18-hour days, but I seemed to have been driven to be successful because of my poor childhood. Finally, in 1976, (I was 42 years old) after much discussion and prayer with my wife, Raydean, I committed myself to downsizing my involvement.

I sold my partnership in Kinney-Clayton and sold all the properties my investment group had purchased. I retained ownership of Clayton's Interiors. This greatly improved things at home and I was able to devote more attention to running just one business.

In 1980, we further simplified our business by buying a building on West Market Street. We moved the fixtures, inventory and employees from Forum Six mall and High Point Road to the West Market Street location. Thanks to a great economy (with a couple of rough years), we grew fast. We praise God for His blessings during these years.

After 35 years of being in business, we decided to sell Clayton Interiors. I was seventy years old and was really struggling with my spinal tumor problem. So, in 2004, two employees bought the business, but not the real estate. We kept the building and leased it to the new owners and other tenants.

One of the reasons we were able to enjoy such rapid growth from 1969 until 1976 was because God blessed us. Another reason was because of the friendship and trust of an up-and-coming young banker named Bill Black.

Starting in 1969, with about $10,000 in cash, we accumulated by 1976 the following: 100% interest in three successful retail stores, 49% interest in three office furniture and supply stores, and 33% interest in an apartment building and several rental houses.

Whenever I needed money for payroll, inventory, or expansion, Bill Black would lend it to me. I always paid him back, either on time or early. Our relationship grew so sound that I could call him on the phone, tell him much I needed, and he would deposit it in my account. He would allow me to come by the bank and sign the papers at my convenience. I rewarded him by placing all our business with his bank.

Another way I financed the growth was to invest my entire salary and bonuses from Kinney-Clayton Company back into the businesses. My personal expenses were paid by my income from Clayton Interiors. I also had good income from Hooper Publishing Company, a franchise I owned which created advertising help for small retail businesses.

In 1975, we joined the Greensboro Country Club. I wanted to do this for several reasons. First, I thought it would be good for our businesses. Second, this club had a very strong tennis program, with excellent tennis courts, and many outstanding tennis players. I had started playing tennis seriously in 1968, and I thought the competition to be found at Greensboro Country Club would help me to improve my tennis skills. Third, since the days I worked as a golf caddy at the Newnan Country Club in my early teen years, I had a dream that one day I would belong to a country club.

This turned out to be a good decision. The amount of new business developed as a direct result of friends at the club was far more than I had anticipated. The new sales gained came from the relationships and not from overt sales approaches. The tennis program helped me improve as a tennis player. I played on the GCC Men's tennis team in competition with other country clubs and tennis clubs. I did well in club tournaments and city tournaments. As I entered my senior years, I qualified to represent Greensboro in the State Senior Games in Raleigh five years in a row. My best showing in city tournaments was in 1994 when I was 60 years old. Because of very strong doubles partners, we won the city championship for men, age 55 and over. In the same tournament, with a younger partner, we won the B Open Division Championship for all ages. In addition, my doubles partner and I advanced to the finals of our age group in the State Senior Games in Raleigh.

I loved playing tennis. In the 36 years I played, tennis provided good exercise, wonderful fellowship with other players, a relief from stress, and exciting competition.

Just as He promised us in the Bible, God has watched over and blessed our family countless times. For example, in the early '90's, Promise Keepers, a well-known men's evangelist organization, organized a Pastor's Conference at the huge Georgia Dome in Atlanta. Over 43,000 pastors attended this five-day event. My wife and I volunteered to go and serve as ushers.

It was a fantastic time of worship, music, and encouragement for this large group of pastors. The team of ushers I worked with all week became pretty well-acquainted with each other. On the last day of the event, we were having lunch together. One of the men suggested we all tell the group what we did for a living. When my turn came, I told the guys that my company supplied one-inch mini-blinds and shades for windows in homes and commercial buildings.

After the meeting, one of the ushers called me aside. He said, "I've watched how you have worshipped God and served these pastors all week. I know it has been a sacrifice for you and your wife to be away from your business all this week." He continued, "I'm from Raleigh and I own over 4000 apartment units. We have several new properties under construction now all over North and South Carolina. I want you to be our exclusive supplier of one-inch mini-blinds. We buy thousands of those blinds every year."

He gave me his business card and we made arrangements to meet at his office the following Monday. His company became a very large purchaser of my products, and it was a pleasant and profitable arrangement for many years. Praise God!!

Shortly after moving to Greensboro in 1964, we joined Lawndale Baptist church. Since we were first married, Raydean and I have always been active in church, usually teaching in the youth department. We continued that tradition of service at Lawndale.

The most satisfying and spiritually rewarding ministry at church was my involvement as Royal Ambassador leader , which spanned over 35 years. This is a missions organization for boys from first through sixth grade. We emphasized salvation, memorizing Bible verses, and learning about missions work, and we made it fun. We scheduled lots of father/son activities including camping, college football games, NASCAR racing, bike hikes, etc. Our R.A. counselors were all carefully selected, dedicated men who loved teaching boys. We could only claim partial credit, but it was very satisfying that from those early years, ten R.A. boys grew up to become full-time pastors, missionaries, or Christian leaders in other jobs. Our son, Alan, was active in the R.A.'s during this time and is now senior pastor of a mega-church in Conroe, Texas with several thousand members.

Serving more than three decades as a deacon at Lawndale was a wonderful blessing. I thank God also for allowing me to serve as Men's Ministry leader for eleven years. Those were years of spiritual growth for me and for other men involved in that ministry.

Both our children, Alan and Leslie, became Christians early in life. They were good students, active in school affairs and especially active in various sports teams at Northwest High School.

After graduation, Leslie attended Rockingham Community College, worked for a short time, and then joined the Navy. It was there that she met and married

Jeff Edwards. They had a son, Josh, who unfortunately died of cancer at age 17. This was an incredibly difficult time for Leslie and Jeff especially, and also for the rest of our family. Leslie now lives in San Diego, and works as a martial arts instructor. This job is her ministry as she teaches her pupils Christian principles and life principles while they are learning martial arts.

Alan and his wife, Joy, have been blessed with three outstanding children, Matthew, 26, Christina, 24, and Michael, 18. Matthew and his lovely wife, Kelly, are missionaries in Peru. Christina is an occupational therapist, and Michael is a senior in high school.

During those days of healing after my operation in 1999, I had a lot of time to think about my family, my experiences at church, my career, and the many ways that God had guided and blessed me and my family. But my thoughts kept coming back to what my life was going to be like sentenced to a wheelchair. I had always been very active and involved in many different activities. My mind was still busy and alert, I felt great, but my wheelchair really slowed me down. I realized that I must develop more patience and experience a renewing of my mind. I knew that I needed to get deeply involved in God's Word to accomplish this.

Gradually my thoughts changed from negative to more positive ones. I spent quite a lot of time reading the Bible and praying. I've been a Christian for over 60 years and have read the Bible a lot, but I never realized how much the Bible has to say about suffering. Here are some of those verses.

"That is why we never give up. Though our bodies are dying, our inner strength in the Lord is growing every day" (2 Corinthians 4:16, TLB).

"Shall we receive only pleasant things from the hand of God and never receive anything unpleasant?" (Job 2:10, TLB)

Does God want what's best for us? He certainly does. But that doesn't always mean a life of comfort. When I think about spending the rest of my life in a wheelchair, I remember Paul was bound by chains in a Roman prison. He wrote, "For it has been granted to you on behalf of Christ not only to believe on Him, but also to suffer for Him" (Philippians 1:29, TLB).

I began searching and praying about what God's will for me was and how I might serve Him, even in a wheelchair. I've learned some important truths about the ways a handicapped person like me can glorify God. One way is to maintain my loyalty to God even when facing difficult trials. God is worth serving even when the going gets tough.

I have begun to see that the loss of my ability to walk helps me to understand and have empathy for people in similar conditions. I am able to relate to people I would not have been able to understand before. Jesus Himself suffered at the crucifixion. We have a Savior who can help others when they are suffering. Since Jesus endured hardship so He could relate to those who suffer, we should do no less.

People who have experienced serious losses and suffering are sometimes turned off by the testimonies of attractive, healthy Christians. It would be difficult not to think, "This guy probably never felt real pain. What does he know about life's problems?" People like this will often listen to a person who also has difficulties.

I am learning that my wheelchair is more of a tool than a tragedy. If I can consistently display genuine joy, peace, and enthusiasm as I go about in my chair, some people are curious. Sometimes it causes people to realize that their problems aren't so bad after all. Often a person will confide in me about a difficulty they are dealing with. It gives me a great opportunity to encourage them and to tell them about "The God who gives you hope and keeps you happy and full of peace as you believe in him" (Romans 15:13, TLB).

Why am I in a wheelchair? The Bible is full of good things that can come from handicaps and suffering.

1. Pain and discomfort get our minds off temporary things and force us to think about God. We read the Bible more and pay closer attention. We pray more.
2. Adversities deflate pride and teach us to depend on God. That helps us to know God better.
3. Physical problems give us the opportunities to praise God even when it's hard. This pleases Him and proves how great He is to inspire such loyalty.

I sometimes wonder what I would be doing today if the tumor had not attacked my body and eventually sentenced me to a wheelchair. I couldn't understand at first why God would allow it, but I understand now. He has gotten more glory through my handicap than through my health. I have learned that if God chooses to answer my prayers and heal me, I should thank him for it. But if He has chosen not to, I thank Him anyway—He has His reasons. We will never totally understand God. "O, the depth of the riches both of the wisdom and knowledge of God! How unsearchable are His judgments, and His ways past finding out! For who hath known the mind of the Lord or who hath been His counselor" (Romans 11:33-34, KJV).

One thing I have determined is that I will finish strong with what I have left. As I finish strong, most of it will be in service to the members of Lawndale Baptist Church in Greensboro, North Carolina, where I have been a member since 1964. Our pastor is Dr. Joe Giaritelli, an incredibly gifted man of God. His wife, P.J., is also gifted but in other ways, leading the women of the church, working with the choir, drama, and much more. We have the most outstanding group of associate pastors to be found anywhere. My wife, Raydean, and I work most closely with Rodney Navey and Marion Boling. We serve in the Senior Adult Ministry and as leaders of a Sunday morning Life Journey Group for young couples. We also serve as marriage counselors and mentors for married couples. We are active in three Bible studies each week, and we try to encourage other people and build bridges wherever we are—the YMCA, the grocery store, the gas station, the senior center, etc. We also have an extensive card ministry for the sick, the discouraged, the hospitalized, and those with birthdays or anniversaries.

Anything we do for the Kingdom of God has eternal value. Too often we disqualify ourselves from serving. We express sentiments such as: I am too old, past my prime, who wants to listen to someone like me? God has no mandatory retirement age. He is still looking for someone, anyone who will say "Here am I, Lord, send me." Finishing strong with what you have left is by choice, not by chance. I trust the stories of faith and determination in this book will help you and strengthen you as you finish your race. May we all be able to say with the Apostle Paul, "I have fought the good fight, I have finished the race, I have kept the faith. Now there is in store for me the crown of righteousness, which the Lord, the righteous Judge, will award to me on that day—and not only to me, but also to all who have longed for His appearing" (2 Timothy 4:7,8 TLB).

Favorite Bible Verses

The following are some Bible verses that have been comforting and encouraging to me over the years. I encourage you to refer to these when you feel the need.

Philippians 3:7, TLB - "But all these things that I once thought very worthwhile—now I've thrown them all away so that I can put my trust and hope in Christ Jesus."

Philippians 3:13-14, TLB - "I am still not all I should be, but I am bringing all my energies to bear on this one thing: forgetting the past and looking forward to what lies ahead, I strain to reach the end of the race and receive the prize for which God is calling us up to heaven, because of what Christ Jesus did for us."

Hebrews 2:18, TLB - "For since He Himself has now been through suffering and temptation, He knows what it's like when we suffer and are tempted, and He is wonderfully able to help us."

2 Corinthians 1:3-4, TLB - "What a wonderful God we have—He is the Father of our Lord Jesus Christ, the source of every mercy, and the one who so wonderfully comforts and strengthens us in our hardships and

trials. And why does He do this? So that when others are troubled, needing our sympathy and encouragement, we can pass on to them this same help and comfort God has given us."

2 Corinthians 12:9-10, TLB – "Now I am glad to boast about how weak I am; I am glad to be a living demonstration of Christ's power, instead of showing off my own power and abilities. Since I know it is all for Christ's good, I am quite happy about "the thorn" and about insults and hardships, persecutions and difficulties; for when I am weak, then I am strong—the less I have, the more I depend on Him."

1 Peter 4:12-13, TLB- "Don't be bewildered or surprised when you go through the fiery trials ahead. Instead, be really glad because these trials will make you partners with Christ in His suffering."

Colossians 3:2, TLB - "Let heaven fill your thoughts; don't spend your time worrying about things down here."

Romans 5:3-4, TLB – "We can rejoice, too, when we run into problems and trials, for we know that they are good for us. They help us learn to be patient, and patience develops strength of character in us, and helps us trust God more each time we use it until finally our hope and faith are strong and steady."

Philippians 1:12, TLB - "And I want you to know this, dear brothers: everything that has happened to me here has been a great boost in getting out the good news concerning Christ."

2 Corinthians 4:8-10, 15-18, TLB - "We are pressed on every side by trouble, but not crushed and broken. We are perplexed because we don't know why things happen as they do, but we don't give up and quit. We are hunted down, but God never abandons us. We get knocked down, but we get up again and keep going. These bodies of ours are constantly facing death just as Jesus did; so it is clear to all that it is only the living Christ within (who keeps us safe). These sufferings of ours are for your benefit. And the more of you who are won to Christ, the more there are to thank Him for His great kindness, and the more the Lord is glorified. That is why we never give up. Though our bodies are dying, our inner strength in the Lord is growing every day. These troubles and sufferings of ours are, after all, quite small and won't last very long. Yet this short time of distress will result in God's richest blessings upon us forever and ever. So we do not look at what we can see right now, the troubles all around us, but we look forward to the joys in heaven which we have not yet seen. The troubles will soon be over, but the joys to come will last forever."

LaVergne, TN USA
13 February 2011
216357LV00002B/1/P

Savoring the Moments

True Stories of Happiness, Sadness, and Everything in Between

CHARLES SACCHETTI